THE LEVITICAL OFFERINGS

The Levitical Offerings

by
DR. JOHN BOYD

PRECIOUS SEED PUBLICATIONS

First published as a series of articles in
Precious Seed Magazine 1965-66

ISBN: 978-1-871642-27-8

Printed in China

Contents

Introduction

This booklet was first published as a series of articles in *Precious Seed* magazine over the years 1965-66. They are now published in this form that they might stimulate a new generation to study this important area of typical truth.

Paul, in writing to the believers in Rome, taught them: 'Whatsoever things were written aforetime were written for our learning, that we through patience and comfort of the scriptures might have hope', Rom. 15. 4. Whilst this verse relates to all scripture rather than the portion considered by Dr. Boyd, it is as relevant to his study as it is to those other portions of the word of God.

The Levitical Offerings afford a study of immense importance as they teach us so much concerning the significance and scope of the work of Christ on the cross at Calvary. How important to deepen our appreciation of the work of the Lord Jesus Christ!

Terminology employed by the New Testament writers is often derived from the offerings. In the Epistle to the Philippians, for example, Paul speaks of being 'offered upon the sacrifice and service of your faith', Phil. 2. 17. So much of the Epistle to the Hebrews is better understood by referring to rituals such as those laid down in respect to these offerings.

Thus, in this booklet there is that which will draw out our affection to Christ, reveal something of the character of our God, challenge our spiritual life and testimony and deepen our understanding of the word of God.

On behalf of Precious Seed Publications

John Bennett
June 2009

The Levitical Offerings

1. GENERAL REMARKS

When God delivered the children of Israel from the bondage of Egypt, He made choice of them above all the peoples of the earth, Amos 3. 2, and brought them unto Himself, Exod. 19. 4-6. Provided they kept His covenant, they would be His peculiar treasure and they would manifest this by becoming unto God a kingdom of priests and a holy nation. Now, a priest is one who draws near to God, Exod. 19. 22. It may be that as a 'kingdom of priests' God intended Israel to act as mediator between Him and the nations, as will be realized in the millennium, Zech. 8. 13, 23. Again, it may mean that God wanted the children of Israel to be His subjects and as individuals to draw near to Him; possibly the latter is the true meaning. With this end in view, God gave Israel the ceremonial law with its multiplicity of offerings, that they might know how to approach Him correctly.

There seems to have been a priesthood in Israel before the exodus from Egypt, but not from the house of Aaron, Exod. 5. 3; 19. 22. These priests had been chosen by the Israelites themselves. God prohibited them from approaching Mount Sinai, 19. 24, thus indicating that He was about to set them aside, and establish instead the Levitical priesthood.

This present study is concerned with the functioning of this Levitical priesthood, vested particularly in the sons of Aaron. It is our purpose to consider how they functioned and how the various details of their offerings pointed forward to that great focus of all history and of all sacrifices, the work of Christ on the cross – since all scripture speaks of Him, John 5. 39. We shall note also how the offerings provide instruction for the walk and service of the believer today. This study demands that we appreciate exactly what the various offerings meant to the children of Israel themselves. How did they regard these instructions from God?

What did they express by their gifts? What did God wish to teach them?

The offerings are a parable for our instruction, but before we can learn its lesson we must first thoroughly understand the parable itself. We must know the **literal meaning** before we can appreciate the **typical teaching**. If we can comprehend something of the needs of the Israelite supplied by the many Levitical offerings, we will realize something of the greatness of the sacrifice of Christ on our behalf. His sacrifice took the place of all their offerings and has accomplished what all the blood that flowed from Jewish altars could never achieve. He put away sin by the sacrifice of Himself, Heb. 9. 26.

Let us then take up our position alongside the Israelite of 1490 B.C., uninfluenced at first by the later knowledge that the New Testament imparts. These offerings were appointed by God as a means of approach to Him. Whilst they did not render perfect the worshipper in the sight of God, they formed a basis for atonement – a going on with God. Their great variety made the Israelite realize his shortcomings and the great distance between God and himself.

We first examine the various technical terms used in connection with the Levitical offerings and what these terms meant to the Israelite.

1. General Terms

Corban, lit. something brought to God – a general expression for the bringing of an offering. It was used in connection with all the offerings except the trespass offering. The King James Version rendering 'offering' is rendered 'oblation' in the Revised Version. The Septuagint equivalent is the Greek *doron*, a gift; see Mark 7. 11. This is the word used of the gifts of the princes of Israel, Num. 7. 3, and suggests that the Levitical offerings were holy gifts.

Zebach, lit. a slaughtered animal, usually translated in the King James Version as 'sacrifice'. It is frequently used in association with the peace offering, e.g., a sacrifice of a peace offering, Lev. 3. 1. The Septuagint usually translates it *thusia* – something slain, but the Greek word covers a wider field than the Hebrew, being used also of the meal offering.

2. Blood Offerings

'Olah, lit. what ascends, that is, something ascending to God. The King James Version usually gives 'burnt offering'. The Septuagint translates it often by *holokautoma* – what is wholly burnt. Thus, two fundamental ideas are suggested by these titles: (1) worship ascending to God; and (2) the sacrifice was all for God.

Shelem, lit. a salvation offering, for deliverance either received or expected. The King James Version rendering is 'peace offering'. The Septuagint translates it by *thusia soteriou*, lit. an offering of deliverance. Three distinctions are seen in this offering, according to its purpose, 7. 12-16: (1) as a thanksgiving – for salvation received; (2) for a vow – an offering on the fulfilment of an expected salvation, 22. 21; Acts 21. 26; and (3) a voluntary peace offering – simple rejoicing with God. The fundamental idea in the offering was that of giving thanks to God.

Chattath, lit. an offering for missing the mark. The King James Version rendering is 'sin offering'. Sin and the sin offering are often expressed by the same Hebrew word, see Lev. 4. 3, where 'sin' and 'sin offering' are the same word. The Septuagint translates it by *hamartia*, sin. The fundamental idea in this offering was that of reconciliation to God.

Asham, lit. an offering for one guilty of a fault, Lev. 5. 6. The King James Version renders it 'trespass offering', and the Revised Version 'guilt offering'. Trespass is a wrong done, sin is the doing of it. The trespass is the stain left. This distinction is well seen in Leviticus chapter 4 verse 3 RV, where the priest is said to have sinned so as to bring guilt upon the people, see also Num. 5. 6, 7. The same Hebrew word is sometimes rendered 'trespass' and 'trespass offering'. It is used of: (1) guilt – arising from the wrong done; (2) the debt; (3) the compensation for the debt; and (4) the sacrifice for the debt – that which sets the offerer free. The Septuagint translates it by *plemmeleia*, lit. out of tune – the false note that spoils the harmony. The fundamental idea in this offering was giving satisfaction to God and to man.

3. Bloodless Offerings

Minchah, lit. what was apportioned, that is, to God. It is first found in Genesis chapter 4 verses 3 and 5, describing the offerings of Cain and Abel. It is used of a present, Gen. 32. 13. The Hebrew word is used for: (1) an offering in general; (2) a present; (3) the technical term for 'meat offering' KJV, or 'meal offering' RV. The Septuagint translates it by *thusia*, a sacrifice, something offered to God, but not necessarily slain. The fundamental idea in this offering was the presentation to God of His portion.

Nesek, lit. what is poured out, or poured upon another offering. The King James and Revised Versions both render it 'drink offering'. It is used for: (1) drink offerings in general, for example, of oil, 35. 14, of blood, Ps. 16. 4; and (2) the technical term for the 'drink offering' of wine poured on burnt offerings and peace offerings (but never on a sin offering or trespass offering). The Septuagint translates it by *sponde*, what is poured out. The fundamental idea behind this offering was giving joy to God.

4. Ritual Offerings

The following terms, not offerings in themselves, are used to describe the treatment of part of the offerings.

Terumah, lit. something raised, or lifted up as a present. It is used of: (1) an offering presented to God, for example, when Israel was told to give to God the things necessary for the construction of the tabernacle, Exod. 25. 2; and (2) the technical term for the raising toward heaven of the shoulder of the peace offering, afterwards eaten by the priest, Lev. 7. 32. The King James Version gives 'heave offering'. The Septuagint translates it by *aphairema*, what is taken away. The fundamental idea behind this ritual was the reception from God of that which was first offered to Him. It was also an acknowledgement that God's throne is in heaven.

Tenuphah, lit. a waving, what is waved to and fro. The King James Version uses 'wave offering'. It is used of: (1) an offering of gold to God, Exod. 35. 22; and (2) the technical term for waving the breast of the peace offering, Lev. 7. 30, the ram of consecration, 8. 27, the leper's trespass offering, 14. 12, the sheaf of firstfruits, 23. 11, and the loaves at Pentecost, 23. 17. The Septuagint translates it *aphorisma*, what is set apart. The fundamental idea was the display before God of what was appreciated. Possibly it symbolized the giving of the offering first to God (because it was waved toward the altar), and then its transference to the priest from God (because it was waved away from the altar). Some see in it a suggestion that God is everywhere, just as the heave offering acknowledges that He is in heaven. Or, was it waved for man to see? Compare the ritual of the jealousy trial, Num. 5. 25.

In these offerings only the best should be given to God. It had also to be mature and physically perfect, Mal. 1. 8.

Six Main Offerings

There were six main offerings prescribed in the ceremonial law:

   (1) the burnt offering;
   (2) the meal offering;
   (3) the peace offering;
   (4) the sin offering;
   (5) the trespass offering;
   (6) the drink offering.

Different combinations of these offerings were used in the various services of the tabernacle, for example,

   (1) the daily offerings;
   (2) the offerings at the set feasts, Lev. 23;
   (3) the offerings in connection with special occasions, namely, the consecration of the priests, the Nazarite vow, the cleansing of the leper, the person defiled with an issue, the parturient woman, and the jealousy trial.

These offerings were designated 'the bread of God' because they consisted of that which was the food of the Israelite, but which instead of eating he offered to God, 21. 6. They were also called 'the holy things of the children of Israel', 22. 15.

These six main offerings are divided into three groups: (1) the sweet savour offerings, namely the burnt and the peace offerings; (2) the expiatory offerings – the sin and the trespass offerings; and (3) the supplementary offerings – the meal and the drink offerings, both of which were added to other offerings. The meal offering is also included amongst the sweet savour offerings.

We are impressed by the multiplicity and comprehensiveness of these offerings. They reminded Israel of the complexity of their relations with *Jehovah*, of His absolute holiness, and their own sinfulness. Conscious of their uncleanness and defilement, they craved mercy, forgiveness and reconciliation through the offerings. In them, they expressed their need of atonement and their desire to have access to God; they realized what calling on God demanded, and what fellowship with Him meant. They thus acknowledged that all that they had they owed to God, and sought in return to yield themselves fully to Him.

How all this magnifies the grace of God in Christ! All these offerings find their anti-type in the Lord Jesus Christ. His one sacrifice at Calvary covered all the requirements of these multitudinous offerings; yea more, His sacrifice far exceeded these. It needed no repetition; it was once for all; it perfected them that were thereby sanctified; it stands out in contrast to the continually recurring Levitical offerings, which, so far from removing sins, were constant reminders to the children of Israel of their sinfulness. Let us also appreciate Christ as the Offerer and as the Priest. As the Offerer, He offered Himself without spot to God, Heb. 9. 14; 10. 5-10. As the Priest, He offered one sacrifice, and entered heaven by means of His own blood, Heb. 9. 12-14; 10. 11-12; 12. 24.

May we become more conscious daily of our sinful tendencies, of the holiness of God, and what drawing near to Him entails. Let us rejoice that the sacrifice of Christ has met all God's demands, enabling us to draw near to God in full assurance of faith.

2. THE BURNT OFFERING

Burnt offerings were presented to God long before the Levitical economy, by Noah, Gen. 8. 20, by Abraham, Gen. 22. 2, and by Job, Job 1. 5. They were offered also by the heathen to their gods, for example, by the king of Moab, 2 Kgs. 3. 27, and by Balak, Num. 23. 3. The main conception in a burnt offering is that there is someone above, whom the offerer wished to propitiate. The essential meaning of the Hebrew word *olah* is that of something ascending.

In scripture, the term 'burnt offering' is used of: (1) any animal sacrificed and burned with fire to cause a savour to ascend to God; and (2) the specific Levitical offering prescribed by God to indicate how the Israelite should approach Him in worship. This study has to do exclusively with this latter use. These offerings were not intended to be mainly for expiation. Other offerings dealt with the sins of the Israelite, this one more with his approach to God in worship. The Levitical burnt offering is divided into two groups: (1) the statutory burnt offerings – laid down as obligatory by God; and (2) voluntary burnt offerings – offered by individuals over and above the statutory offerings.

The Statutory Burnt Offerings

God ordained that these should be offered on many and varied occasions. The nature and number of animals were specified, differing according to the time and the purpose for which they were offered.

A burnt offering was offered twice every day, one lamb each morning and evening; this was called the continual burnt offering, Exod. 29. 42. It was basic, and had to be offered apart from any other special or voluntary offering. The fire of this continual burnt offering was always kept burning, the ashes being cleared away each morning. The evening burnt offering was on the fire all night. Every morning the fire was replenished with wood in preparation for the day's offerings.

Each Sabbath, two lambs were offered for 'the burnt offering of every sabbath', Num. 28. 9-10.

On the first day of each month a special burnt offering was presented, consisting of two young bullocks, one ram and seven lambs, 28. 11.

The seven annual feasts of Jehovah each had its quota of burnt offerings:

(1) on the Passover many oxen were sacrificed,
2 Chron. 30. 24;
(2) on each of the seven days of the feast of unleavened bread two bullocks, one ram and seven lambs were offered,
Num. 28. 24;
(3) on the feast of firstfruits one he-lamb, Lev. 23. 12;
(4) on the feast of Pentecost one young bullock, two rams and seven lambs, 23. 18;
(5) on the feast of trumpets one bullock, one ram and seven lambs, Num. 29. 2;
(6) for the day of atonement two burnt offerings were commanded, one for Aaron and one for the people,
Lev. 16. 24; and
(7) during the feast of tabernacles a different-sized burnt offering was prescribed for each of the eight days of the feast,
Num. 29. 13 ff.

Burnt offerings also formed part of the ritual of many other functions of the Levitical economy; for example,

(1) the consecration of the priests, Lev. 8. 18, of the people,
9. 2, and of the Levites, Num. 8. 12;
(2) at the dedication of the altar, 7. 87, and of the temple,
1 Kgs. 8. 64;
(3) as part of the cleansing rites of the parturient woman,
Lev. 12. 6, of the leper, 14. 19, of the person with an issue,
15. 15. of the defiled Nazarite, Num. 6. 11; and
(4) on the completion of a vow, 13. 3 RV, or of a Nazarite separation, 6. 14.

These statutory burnt offerings were given by God to Israel to enable them to keep in contact with Him. He wanted them ever to seek His habitation, Exod. 29. 42. They were a constant reminder to His people that God was over all in heaven; that 'he is, and that he is a rewarder of them that diligently seek him', Heb. 11. 6. To God they presented a sweet savour of rest; He found satisfaction in them as a source of delight.

In them, God sets forth His desire for the believer to be continually drawing near to Him in worship. The Lord taught that men ought always to pray. Paul's theme so often was 'continue instant in prayer'. Like the burnt offerings in the set feasts, God in His wisdom has given us the Lord's supper as a recurring reminder to approach His presence, there to make much of His Son. We then present the Lord Jesus Christ as our burnt offering, seeing in Him the One whose offering makes us acceptable to God; whose blood has cleansed us and made us fit to be in God's presence; whose perfections the Father delights to hear mentioned as on each occasion we proclaim the Lord's death.

The Voluntary Burnt Offerings

In addition to the statutory burnt offerings, God ordained that an individual Israelite could, of his own free will, present a burnt offering, Lev. 1. 2 ff; 22. 18. The ceremonial law prescribed what should be offered on such an occasion, and how it had to be presented. The choice of the oblation was fourfold, and was left to the offerer, according to his appreciation or to his ability to provide. The offering must be valuable; he may not offer what had cost him nothing, 2 Sam. 24. 24. He could bring either a bullock, a lamb or a goat – these were animals of value to a rich man. Provision was also made for the poor man in that a turtle-dove or a pigeon would be accepted. A high standard of perfection was ever demanded in the animal chosen; it had to be a male without blemish – God would accept only the best, Mal. 1. 8.

This offering indicated a desire of the Israelite to approach God, to acknowledge full dependence upon Him and to express just how much he appreciated God – the greater his offering, the greater his appreciation. It was an expression of the worship of his heart. The animal was accepted for him, Lev. 1. 4; it represented the consecration and self-surrender of the whole man to God. As a result, the man was accepted by God, although it could never be a substitute for obedience to God, 1 Sam. 15. 22, neither could it take the place of a broken contrite heart, Ps. 51. 16-17.

The Ritual

The ritual of the burnt offering followed a very clearly prescribed pattern. Set out as for a voluntary burnt offering in Leviticus chapter 1, it is possible that this pattern applied very largely to the statutory offerings also.

First, the animal had to be presented at the door of the tabernacle, at which stood the brazen altar upon which alone the offering had to be burned, Lev. 17. 8-9; no other altar would suffice. It is significant to notice that the brazen altar was sometimes called the 'place of the burnt offering', Lev. 4. 29. The offerer laid (lit. leaned) his hand on the head of the offering, thereby to acknowledge his identification with and dependence upon it. In offering the animal, he offered himself to God. He depended upon its acceptance by God, that with it an atonement might be made for him.

Secondly, the offerer killed the animal and shed its blood, which the priest took and sprinkled round about upon the brazen altar. The sprinkling of the blood signified that the life had been given to God and thus atonement was made for the offerer. The Hebrew word translated atonement means 'to cover'. The Greek word in the Septuagint implies that God is graciously disposed towards the offerer. Thus, when the burnt offering was slain, its blood on the altar covered that which caused displeasure to God. Some have differentiated between the atonement of the burnt offering and that of the sin offering, in that the former had to do with the wrong thoughts or designs of the Israelite, and the latter with his wrong acts.

Thirdly, the offerer prepared the carcass of the animal for the altar. He removed the skin, the only part which was not burnt, and which became the property of the priest, 7. 8. Next he cut the flesh of the animal into suitable pieces; these the priest placed on the altar, after the inwards and legs had been washed with water so that nothing unclean would be attached to the offering. Then, all was burned on the altar by the priest. The word 'burn' here implies 'to emit fragrance'; it was for God. This word is always used for burning on the brazen altar and is different from that used for burning the sin offering outside the camp, Lev. 4. 12, where it means simply to set on fire. In some offerings the offerer and the priest shared a part, but in the burnt offering all went to God; the sacrifice was wholly burnt as a sweet savour to God.

Provision was also made for an offerer who by reason of poverty could only bring a dove or a pigeon. As in the case of an animal, he presented the bird to God, but to the priest was given the task of killing it. This he did by wringing off the head, and placing it on the altar. The blood was drained out at the side of the altar, thereby to make atonement. It is not clear why God ordained that the priest kill the bird instead of the offerer, except that the quantity of blood would be too small to be caught in a bowl. The crop and the 'filth thereof', 1. 16 RV, were discarded, corresponding to the washing of the inwards and legs of the animal. The wings were pulled apart, but not separated from the body of the bird; this exposed all the parts equally. Then the whole was burned on the altar, causing a sweet savour to ascend to God.

The burnt offering had to be accompanied by a meal and a drink offering, but the size of these subsidiary offerings varied with the animal presented as a burnt offering. Num. 15. 3-12. Also trumpets were sounded over the burnt offerings sacrificed at the set feasts, and at the beginning of the months, Num. 10. 10.

Three main features are evident in this ritual:

(1) the offering, Lev. 1. 3 – for the offerer's *acceptance with God;*
(2) the killing, Lev. 1. 5 – for the offerer's *atonement before God;*
(3) the burning, Lev. 1. 9 – for the offerer's *adoration of God.*

These facts teach us that the burnt offering, to the Israelite, was essentially an act of worship. This was the method by which he could approach God, expressing his total indebtedness to Him and his dependence upon Him.

The Truth set forth by the Differing Offering

The Israelite offerer portrays the believer today in his desire to approach God; by faith, he presents the Lord Jesus Christ as a burnt offering. In His sojourn on earth, the Lord showed His suitability, for He was sinless and without blemish; He is accepted by God, for in Him was the Father's delight as One ever doing the will of God. The different animals offered under the Levitical economy suggest different appreciations of Christ. Even the least instructed believer – one young in the faith – can offer his dove-like appreciation of Him. Mature believers – those well instructed in the word – present Him in the magnitude of His perfection as represented by the bullock.

The believer is now accepted by God in all the acceptability of Christ, 'He hath made us accepted in the beloved', Eph. 1. 6; 'we are in him that is true', 1 John 5. 20. In the will of God, 'we are sanctified through the offering of the body of Jesus Christ once for all', Heb. 10. 10. But, as in the case of the Israelite, he cannot approach God unless conscious of a whole-hearted obedience to Him – in brokenness and contrition of spirit, lifting up holy hands, without wrath and disputing, 1 Tim. 2. 8 RV.

The removal of the skin and the cutting of the animal into pieces typify the display of the secret perfections of Christ's inner life.

The work of the priest in connection with the burnt offering sets forth the work of the Lord Jesus Christ as our Great High Priest. He pleads the merit of His precious blood. Fire is emblematic of the Holy Spirit, Acts 2. 3; by the Spirit He displayed before God and demonstrated to the believer His manifold perfections as evoked by His experience on Calvary.

The death of Christ, too, forms the basis of the believer's approach to God. He has 'boldness to enter into the holiest by the blood of Jesus', Heb. 10. 19; 'now in Christ Jesus we who sometimes were far off are made nigh by the blood of Christ', Eph. 2. 13. In the consecration of the priests, Exod. 29. 21, atonement was made by the blood of the burnt offering being sprinkled on them, covering the displeasure that their evil minds had caused God. In like manner, the believer's heart has been sprinkled from an evil conscience by the blood of Christ, fitting him to draw near to God, Heb. 10. 22.

On the cross, we see Christ's perfections displayed before God for His appreciation; let us look at some of these. There we see His love, which 'to the utmost was tried, but firmly endured as a rock'; His obedience to the Father's will; His grace in humbling Himself to 'death, even the death of the cross'; His determination to carry out God's great plan; His ability to accomplish this task, to endure the cross, to bear the curse; His delight to provide salvation for man; His desire to glorify the Father. All these, and more, the fires of Calvary accentuated and caused God to appreciate them in wondrous profusion.

How willingly then God accepts into His presence the believer on the grounds of such an offering! By faith, we approach God now in the name of Christ; in a future day we shall stand before God in reality, in virtue of what Christ is and what He has wrought.

3. THE MEAL OFFERING

The second offering prescribed for the Israelite in the ceremonial law in Leviticus is the meal offering. The Hebrew term *minchah* is usually translated in the King James Version as meat offering, since the offering consisted mainly of what was the food of the people. Luther rendered it 'food offering'. In 1611 A. D., 'meat' meant food in general, but the revisers changed the name to meal offering to mark the distinction between this offering and the various animal sacrifices, cf. Acts 2. 46, 'meat' KJV, and 'food' RV.

The Hebrew word *minchah* means, literally, that which is apportioned. Its first occurrence in scripture is in Gen. 4. 3-5, where it is used of the offerings brought by Cain and Abel to God. Each brought his *minchah* as an acknowledgement of God's provision for him, with a desire for its continuance. God had respect to Abel's offering, but not to Cain's. No doubt Abel's was the best that he could bring – 'the firstling of the flock, and the fat thereof', cf. Mal. 1. 8. On the other hand, Cain's did not rise to God's expectation and God did not respect it. It is used again of the present which Jacob prepared to appease Esau's wrath and to seek his favour, Gen. 32. 20. It is also used of the present that Joseph's brethren gave him as a token of their homage and gratitude for past favours, Gen. 43. 26. It was a recognition of Joseph's dignity and authority. *Minchah* is also used in the later Old Testament books to denote any kind of offering, grouping them all together under this general term, 1 Sam. 3. 14; 1 Kgs. 18. 29; Mal. 1. 13.

In Leviticus 2, we have this term, *minchah*, used of a specific offering ordained by God for the children of Israel, reminding them that they owed all their sustenance to God. In effect, God said to the Israelite, 'If you wish to acknowledge your indebtedness to Me, I will show you exactly what I require'. He gave Moses detailed requirements for such an offering, that it might be accepted by Him, and that Israel might not, like Cain, be angry at God's non-acceptance of their present. Thus, the *minchah* was the portion given back to God by the Israelites in recognition of His greatness and as an acknowledgement of His provision for their material needs. Being food, it indicated especially God's provision for the sustenance of life. Inherent in it is the idea of remembrance, Lev. 2. 2; Num. 5. 15 RV. It was a sweet-savour offering, presented that God might receive satisfaction from it. Its offering was an act of worship, of gratitude and of petition for future blessings.

A meal offering was also subsidiary to the regular offerings, namely the daily morning and evening sacrifices, the Sabbath offerings and the various festival offerings. These subsidiary offerings differ somewhat from what is set forth in Leviticus chapter 2, in that they consisted merely of prescribed quantities of fine flour mixed with oil, the amount varying with the animal offered, Num. 15. 4-10. The meal offering of Leviticus chapter 2 was offered by private individuals; for example, at the consecration of the priests and Levites, Lev. 6. 20, at the end of the Nazarite vow, Num. 6. 15, and for cleansing of the leper, Lev. 14. 20.

In common with the other sweet-savour oblations, it pointed to Christ who gave Himself for us, an offering to God for a sweet-smelling savour, Eph. 5. 2. The incarnation and the life of Christ were necessary to the accomplishment of His propitiatory death. This fact, taught in the compulsory association of the burnt and meal offerings, points to the latter as a type of the life and service of Christ. It is not, as in the case of the burnt offering, the laying down of His life in death, but His life as lived for God.

In presenting Christ to God as his burnt offering the believer appreciates Him *also* as the perfect anti-type of the meal offering. In it the Lord is presented as the One who perfectly met the requirements of God; the One whom God sent to provide for the sustenance of our spiritual life; the One who was 'the living bread which came down from heaven: if any man eat of this bread, he shall live for ever', John 6. 51. We feed on Christ, and recognize how His life, lived here amongst men, was necessary for our blessing.

The Ingredients

For the Israelite, three ingredients were essential in the meal offering: (1) flour; (2) oil; and (3) frankincense, Lev. 2. 1. Each has a typical import.

Flour, the result of the grinding of wheat (a reducing process for the grain) portrays the humiliation of Christ in coming into manhood. Equal with God, He made Himself of no reputation, being made in the likeness of men, Phil. 2. 7. Fine flour is specified. It indicates the perfection of the humanity of Christ and the evenness of His character, every attribute being in perfect balance. The absence of lumps suggests that in Him no graces outshone any other.

Oil is an emblem of the Holy Spirit, the Spirit that possessed Christ without measure, John 3. 34; He was ever full of the Spirit, and was constantly led of the Spirit.

Frankincense, the most fragrant of balsams, points to the fragrance of the life of Christ – a life that ever pleased the Father. 'All thy garments smell of myrrh, and aloes, and cassia', Ps. 45. 8. All His habits produced a sweet-smelling savour.

Every meal offering must also be seasoned with salt, called the salt of the covenant, Lev. 2. 13. Salt was commonly used in the ratification of a covenant, 2 Chron. 13. 5. This teaches that the meal offering, in common with the other offerings, was in the nature of an acknowledgement of God's covenant with Israel and points to Christ and the new covenant. Salt, an ingredient which restrains corruption, also points to the life of the Lord Jesus Christ being always well-seasoned, with no corruption of speech or thought.

On the other hand, neither leaven nor honey should be offered with the meal offering. While making food palatable, each in its own way tended to corruption. Leaven, typical of malice and wickedness, 1 Cor. 5. 8, was not found in Christ; 'in Him is no sin', 1 John 3. 5. Honey, being natural sweetness, suggests personal glory and that which appeals to the flesh, Prov. 25. 27. Christ sought not His own glory, but that of the Father, John 7. 18.

The Ritual

The ritual connected with this offering is set forth in Leviticus chapter 2 verses 2-3. The offering must be presented to the priest and a handful taken out of the flour and oil; this, together with all the frankincense, was burnt on the altar. Three things are said of the portion thus burned: (1) it was a memorial – it would remind the Israelite of his indebtedness to God; (2) it was an offering made by fire, literally, a firing – it would be consumed by the fire to indicate that it had been devoted to God; and (3) it was a sweet savour – it would give satisfaction to God.

In Leviticus chapter 2, God ordained that three different products may be offered as a meal offering: (1) corn, Lev. 2. 14; (2) dough, 2. 1; and (3) bread, 2. 4. These represent three stages in the preparation of the food of the people, namely: (1) the *corn*, being ears of the new wheat parched on a pan, and rubbed to obtain the roasted grains – a favourite food in harvest, Ruth 2. 14; (2) the *dough*, being the wheat ground into flour and mixed with oil as a batter, and (3) the *flour* baked into bread. This bread was further subdivided into three varieties according to the method of baking: (1) baked in an *oven*; (2) baked on a *flatplate*; and (3) baked by *frying* in oil. Again, the bread baked in the oven may be either in the form of unleavened cakes made from a batter of fine flour and oil, or unleavened wafers over which oil had been poured. In each case, it was a manufactured article that was offered. Thus the Israelite offered the fruit of his own labour to God; he offered a life of service to God.

As with the burnt offering, some meal offerings were compulsory and some voluntary. With the various statutory burnt offerings the Israelite must bring a meal offering, the nature and amount being designated in each case. Fine flour and oil were always specified, but for the various animals offered the amount of flour and oil varied. With a bullock three tenths of an ephah of flour mixed with half an hin of oil were required; with a ram, two tenths of an ephah of flour mixed with a third of an hin of oil; with a lamb one tenth of an ephah of flour mixed with a quarter of an hin of oil, Num. 15. 4-11. These varying quantities suggest different measures of appreciation of God's provision, as the different animals offered in the burnt offerings suggest varying grades of worship. Today, each believer appreciates in a different measure the value of Christ's life and service to God whilst on earth. Much is expected of him to whom much is given.

The Truth set forth by the Offering

What an apt picture of Christ this ritual brings to our hearts! Every time we speak to God of the life of the Lord Jesus Christ we are reminded of our indebtedness to Him for the gift of His Son coming into manhood and bringing untold blessings. We appreciate, too, how His life was lived in perfect devotedness to God. We hear the Saviour say, 'A body hast thou prepared me . . . lo, I come . . . to do thy will, O God', Heb. 10. 5-7. We understand also something of the satisfaction the Father received from that life, as twice we hear the words from heaven, 'This is my beloved Son, in whom I am well pleased', Matt. 3. 17; 17. 5. Thus, we present Christ our meal offering. The believer today would offer his life in service to God, but he is verily conscious that his own service is so inadequate and imperfect that he presents instead the perfect work of Christ. This corresponds to the type set forth in Leviticus chapter 2. The various products present different facets of the life of Christ. In each case the basis of the meal offering is flour made from wheat, the best ingredient that the Israelite used for bread, 1 Chron. 21. 23. The offerer presented only the best fruit – such was the life of Christ.

The different stages in the preparation of the wheat for food suggest different abilities, different experiences, different times spent in God's service. The parched corn reminds us of the Lord's youth at Nazareth, ever subject to the fire of God's holiness. The dough typifies the perfection of the Lord's life of service, the evenness of His character in association with the fullness of the Spirit.

The baking of the bread suggests suffering – not the suffering of Calvary, but the sufferings associated with the Lord's life, His preparation for the altar.

The baking done on the *flatplate* points to the sufferings that Christ endured as He came into contact with the effects of sin in man, when His sorrows became apparent to those around, John 11. 33, 38. The baking in the *frying-pan* points to the open attacks from His enemies whilst He taught, as 'they set themselves vehemently against him', Luke 11. 53 RV margin. The baking in the *oven* indicates the sufferings which He experienced unseen by man, as in the wilderness temptation when He was alone with Satan. Some suggest that the oil mingled with the fine flour represents the incarnation of Christ, conceived by the Holy Spirit, and the wafers anointed with oil the anointing of Christ with the Holy Spirit at His baptism.

One further point remains to be considered, namely, the relationship of the priest to the meal offering. This is dealt with in Leviticus chapter 6 verses 14-18. After he had burned the handful on the altar, the rest was given to him by God for food. The fact that God called this holy, that He ordained it to be baked without leaven and eaten in the holy place, suggests that the whole belonged to God, who gave this remainder to the priest for his sustenance. In this the believer views himself as a priest. When

he offers to God the perfections of Christ's life as his meal offering, he receives from God that which sustains his spiritual life
and satisfies his soul. The believer appreciates just how much he
owes to Christ's activity, even now, on his behalf. He is 'Jesus
Christ the same yesterday, and today, and for ever', Heb. 13. 8.
He is seen in the same characteristics that controlled His work
for men whilst on earth. In what differing degrees do we realize
our indebtedness to Him as our Great High Priest, as Advocate,
as Shepherd and as Friend?

4. THE PEACE OFFERING

In Leviticus chapter 3 God set before Israel His requirements with regard to the peace offering. This is the translation of the Hebrew word *shelem*, coming from a root meaning 'to be safe'. The Revised Version margin sometimes renders it 'thank offering'.

This offering occurs previously in the Old Testament, when a sacrifice to God has been made the occasion of sharing a meal with others. In Genesis chapter 31 verse 54, Jacob and Laban met to make a vow before God and partook of a sacrificial meal. Jethro, in giving thanks to God for His deliverance of Moses and the children of Israel from Egypt, offered a sacrifice and sat down before God to a meal of which he, Aaron and all the elders of Israel took part, Exod. 18. 12. Thus God, as in the cases of the burnt and meat offerings, was pleased to use a sacrificial custom already existing, to correct what was wrong in man's method and to supply what was missing, at the same time pointing forward to the One who should come, the perfect peace offering for man.

The peace offering was a salvation offering, being offered:

(1) as thanksgiving for deliverance, Lev. 7. 12;
(2) on the fulfilment of a vow, when the requested salvation had been realized, 22. 21; and
(3) as a freewill offering, simply expressing the desire to rejoice with God, as did Solomon at the dedication of the temple, 1 Kgs. 8. 63.

The peace offering consisted essentially of an animal slain, part being given to God in firing, part to the priest as food, and the rest eaten as a festive meal. It acknowledged the Israelite's peace with God and indicated his desire to have fellowship with others in expressing the peace he had found in God's deliverance. It was a time of rejoicing because of the peace experienced, cf. Luke 15. 23; moreover, it expressed God's satisfaction in the peace enjoyed.

How beautifully Christ is prefigured in the peace offering! We rejoice in Him who is our peace, Eph. 2. 14; through Him we have peace with God, Rom. 5. 1; He made peace through the blood of His cross, Col. 1. 20. Christ gives us peace, and satisfies our longing hearts, since He has given us the security and certainty of eternal life.

The Offering and the Ingredients

The choice of animal that could be presented as a peace offering was threefold, Lev. 3. 1, 6, 12; the offerer might bring an animal from his herd of oxen, from his flock or from his goats. It must be without blemish, as for the burnt offering. But in Leviticus chapter 22 verse 23, a bullock or a lamb that had something superfluous or lacking could be used for a freewill offering. There was more freedom of choice than in the case of the burnt offering in that he could offer a male or female animal, but there was no provision for offering a pigeon or turtle dove. This liberty is understood when we consider the main purpose of the peace offering – a sacrificial meal. God would permit more latitude that men might more easily – and therefore more frequently – join together with Him in the fellowship of thanksgiving. A small bird could scarcely furnish enough for many to have a share.

This latitude of choice finds a ready explanation in the Person of Christ. As our peace offering, He amply supplies all requirements. God delights in His own appreciation of His Son. As priests, we rejoice to minister to others of the peace found in Christ; as sharers in the feast, we express our gratitude for the salvation Christ has wrought. Meditation on Him produces abundant satisfaction and thanksgiving, and the different-sized animals suggest different comprehensions of His Person.

God ordained that the peace offering should be accompanied by various kinds of cakes:

    (1) unleavened cakes mixed with oil before baking;
    (2) unleavened wafers anointed with oil after baking;
    (3) unleavened cakes baked by frying in oil; and
    (4) cakes of leavened bread.

One each of these four varieties of cakes was taken, the sample heaved unto the Lord, and given to the priest, Lev. 7. 11-14.

In these cakes we see a picture of the service men and women rendered to the Lord when on earth. The *unleavened* cakes (either mixed with, anointed with, or cooked in oil) tell of those holy ones with whom the Spirit dwelt, John 14. 17, and who ministered to Christ on earth, for example: Mary upon whom the Holy Ghost came, Luke 1. 35; John the Baptist, 1. 15, and Simeon, 2. 25-26, both filled with the Holy Spirit. The *leavened* cakes remind us of the publicans and sinners with whom the Saviour ate. Christ was pleased to accept what sinners provided, even the washing of His feet by the sinful woman, Luke 7. 44.

The Ritual

The ritual of the peace offering differed in some respects from that of the burnt offering. The offerer presented his offering at the door of the tabernacle, and laid his hands on its head, thereby acknowledging identification with it. There he killed the animal, the priest taking the blood to sprinkle it on the altar. This followed the pattern for the burnt offering, and reminded the Israelite that the animal took his place in death. Its sprinkled blood made atonement for him.

The offerer then removed some parts of the animal as God's portion. This consisted of:

(1) the veil that covered the intestines, the omentum,
a net-like membrane which is commonly laden with fat;
(2) the fat closely attached to the intestines;
(3) the two kidneys and the fat in which they are buried; and
(4) the caul above the liver. The caul, literally, is the structure that extends from the liver – not so much a lobe of the liver as the lesser omentum, also a net-like membrane which contains fat.

These four portions contain practically all the fat inside the animal. One difference is seen in the case of a lamb. In this animal as found in Palestine, another great depot of fat was the tail, especially the upper part, near the back bone. This, too, must be set aside as God's portion – 'the fat tail entire', Lev. 3. 9 RV. With his own hands the offerer brought all the fat to the priest, who burned it on the altar. It was the Lord's portion; it was an offering made by fire, that is, a firing. It indicated full devotion to God, being wholly consumed by the fire; it was a sweet savour to God, 'All the fat is the Lord's'. It was His 'food of the offering', 3. 16. The burning was the visible evidence of divine appropriation.

The offerer next gave the priest his portions, Lev. 7. 34, the wave breast and the heave shoulder (or thigh, RV). The former was waved to and fro, possibly both by the offerer and the priest. They waved it towards the altar as indicative of being first offered to God, and then back again to represent God giving it back to the priest. In like manner the thigh was heaved up towards God, 10. 15, to acknowledge it as a gift from God to the priest.

Then followed the sacrificial meal. The remainder of the sacrificed animal was given back by God to the offerer and his family. This was eaten before Jehovah, in the place where He chose to put His name, Deut. 12. 11, 18. It was an occasion of rejoicing, v. 7. God was the host, for the animal had been given to Him, and He called on the Israelite to share the animal with Him. Well might he do so with joy! 1 Corinthians chapter 10 verse 18 tells us that the Israelite in thus partaking of this meal was expressing his communion with the altar, that is, with God. The meal must be completed the same day in the case of the thanksgiving peace offering; a vow or a freewill offering might be eaten on the following day also. What remained after these times must be burnt. If any was eaten after the prescribed period, the offering was not accepted; the offerer must bear the consequences by bringing another sacrifice. God desired that there be no delay between the slaying of the animal and partaking of it; the offerer must not have time to forget the death while enjoying its benefits.

Several conditions must be fulfilled in the participation of the peace offering. If the flesh came into contact with anything unclean it must not be eaten, but burnt. All who ate of it must be ceremonially clean. Any who disobeyed this injunction must be excommunicated, being put outside the pale of the protection of the elders of the people, both for life and for property. He would lose the privileges of the covenant people, Lev. 7. 15-21; cf. Gen. 17. 14.

Some prohibitions are also set forth. No fat might be eaten; this was God's portion. Neither was the blood to be eaten, Lev. 7. 22-27; the life of the flesh was in it and it was for atonement, Lev. 17. 11.

The Truth set forth by the Offering

In this ritual we see Christ the Offerer, the Priest and the Offering. As Offerer, Christ presented Himself to God for our salvation, Heb. 10. 7. He gave Himself to be slain for us, that all should share in the satisfaction that His death brought. We, as one with Him and members of His body, appreciate Christ our peace offering today and acknowledge our identification with Him in death, Gal. 2. 20. In the slaying of the animal, we see Christ voluntarily going into death for us. No one took His life from Him; He laid it down of Himself having power to do so, John 10. 18. Next, Christ the Offerer is seen dividing the sacrifice. The fat covering the inwards and the kidneys were given to God. The inward fat and the kidneys tell of the hidden excellence and secret motives that God alone knew and could appreciate in Christ; 'No man knoweth the Son, but the Father', Matt. 11. 27.

The priest's portion – the breast and the right shoulder – tells of Christ finding special satisfaction in some of His own attributes. The breast speaks of affection, the right shoulder of His strength. How often the Lord spoke of His love, for God, for His own and for the world. He spoke, too, of His power – to heal, Luke 5. 17; to teach, 4. 32; to forgive sins, Matt. 9. 6; to die and to rise from the dead, John 10. 18; to overcome the strong one, Satan, Matt. 12. 29; to come in kingly glory, 24. 30. Yea, all power was given unto Him, 28. 18. Christ rejoiced as a strong man to run His course, Ps. 19. 5 RV.

But believers find their joy in Christ as the Offering. We appreciate Him as our peace offering. He was slain for us; His blood was sprinkled on our behalf. God received His portion in that He has appreciated the hidden excellencies of Christ. The Lord Himself has received His portion in seeing of the travail of His soul, thereby being satisfied. There remains therefore the sacrificial meal – the believers' communion with God – a token of friendship and peace with God. This meal today is eaten in God's appointed place and according to His ordinance. God invites the believer to sit at His table and to enjoy fellowship with Him, Heb. 13. 10. This is experienced not merely in the Lord's supper, but in all God's provision for us. We feed on Christ who died for us; His flesh, given for the life of the world, sustains our spiritual life, John 6. 51. This peace offering meal is portrayed for us in our remembrance

of Him, 'the bread which we break is it not a communion of the
body of Christ?', 1 Cor. 10. 16 RV. There we sit in fellowship with
God, rejoicing in what Christ has done for us, Luke 22. 19, 20. The
command to partake of the animal on the day it was slain reminds
us ever to keep fresh in mind the death of Christ; in heaven He is
seen as the freshly slain Lamb, Rev. 5. 6.

Upon bringing a thanksgiving offering, the Israelite had to partake of his portion during that day and night, but if his offering
were for a vow or a freewill offering he could eat of it on the first or
second day, but not on the third day. The 'morning' typifies the
time of Christ's appearing, John 21. 4, the day of our salvation,
Rom. 13. 12; the 'third day' is the day of resurrection, 1 Cor. 15. 4.
Both these figures suggest to us that in the Lord's supper, Christ
is enjoyed as a peace offering whilst awaiting the redemption of
our bodies. The feast is only 'till he come', 1 Cor. 11. 26. Moreover, thanksgiving to God for His Son ought to have a prominent
place in our petitions every time we gather for prayer. Then
we can rejoice with God, and share with Him our varying appreciations of Christ as we express gratitude for the salvation He
has wrought.

The believer should be in the right spiritual condition to partake
of this peace offering. To have communion with Him, we must
not walk in darkness, a life characterized by impurity of motives,
thoughts, words, and deeds, 1 John 1. 6. Cleansing from such
unrighteousness demands the confession of our sins and the
acknowledgement of the cleansing value of the blood of Jesus
Christ His Son, day by day, v. 7.

The believer can also enjoy the priest's portion of the peace offering. As he ministers Christ to others, he himself receives the wave
breast and heave shoulder. He appreciates in a greater degree the
affection of Christ and experiences the power of Christ to meet his
manifold needs. Let us seek more and more this holy service and
its ample rewards.

5. THE SIN OFFERING

The details of the sin offering are found in Leviticus chapter 4 verse 1 to chapter 5 verse 13, with further instructions for the priest in chapter 6 verses 24-30. The Hebrew word translated sin offering is *chattath*, from a root meaning to miss a goal. Sometimes rendered 'sin', that is, the offence, Gen. 18. 20, it is more often used as the technical term for the sin offering, the means by which the sin is covered. Both renderings of the word are found together in Leviticus chapter 4 verse 3.

Unlike the three previous offerings we have considered, there is no mention of the sin offering prior to the giving of the ceremonial law. Genesis chapter 4 verse 7 is no exception. Sin, not the sin offering, lay at Cain's door. The expiation of sin is a new concept, which, although not absent from the burnt and peace offerings, is brought into prominence here. This offering was not seen before Mount Sinai, because through the law came the knowledge of sin. Sin is not imputed where there is no law, Rom. 5. 13.

The purpose of the sin offering is explicitly stated. It was intended to make atonement for an Israelite who had broken God's law, and to restore him to a right relationship with God, Lev. 4. 31. It was not intended for wilful sin; this carried its own punishment. It met the need of a sin committed unwittingly, but which later came to the knowledge of the offender. Examples of what was envisaged are found in Leviticus chapter 5 verses 1-4. When the Israelite became aware of his sin he must confess it, 5. 5, and bring a sin offering, 5. 6. 'Trespass offering' in this verse should rather be rendered 'for his guilt' RV margin. In the animal brought as his substitute, the offerer received the punishment due to his sin.

It is important to note that the sin offering was God's provision for His own people, namely for those who had been sheltered by the blood of the Pascal lamb – for those who had been redeemed from the bondage of Egypt. It was a necessary prelude to other offerings in the Israelite's desire for worship. It developed in him a deep consciousness of sin and guilt, even for sins of which he was not at once aware. All must be atoned for and only by sacrifice.

The Animals Offered

Different animals were required for sin offerings from different ranks of sinners, emphasizing a greater degree of responsibility in some than in others. Four ranks are dealt with:

(1) God's anointed priest (the high priest), 8. 12, must bring a bullock, 4. 3-12;
(2) a similar sacrifice was required for the whole congregation, 4. 13-21;
(3) a ruler must bring a male goat, 4. 22-26; and
(4) one of the common people could bring:
> Either: a female goat, 4. 27-31,
> a female lamb, 4. 32-35,
> two turtledoves or two young pigeons, 5. 7-10,
> or a tenth of an ephah of fine flour, 5. 11-13,

each according to his ability providing what was necessary for the sacrifice.

The high priest must bring a bullock, the same offering as for sin affecting the whole congregation, for his sin brought guilt on all the people. Thus it would seem that the higher the person's rank the more valuable his sin offering must be, indicating that in the sight of God his sin is the more grievous. The application of this today is obvious. Those in high places should be careful lest they sin. Sin is exceeding sinful in those given positions of responsibility in the church, whether elder, teacher, evangelist or Sunday School teacher, Jas. 3. 1. Sin affecting the whole assembly is also most serious in God's sight, cf. Amos 3. 2. Just as Israel, standing in a responsible position towards other nations, must be holy, so the assembly, a centre from which the gospel radiates, must maintain an untarnished reputation.

A ruler, that is the leader of the tribe, was one in a position of secular authority. His sin offering, being of greater value than that of the common people, indicates a higher degree of responsibility to live a holy life. The believer today who holds any post of prominence in the world must likewise watch lest sin mar his testimony before men.

The rank and file of Israel were not exempted from the necessity of bringing a sin offering. Sin in everyone must be atoned for. But

God in His grace made it possible for all, no matter how poor, to have such an opportunity. Four grades of offering were available to the common person, according to his ability to provide. Even the poorest, whose means could rise only to a tenth of an ephah of fine flour, was considered. God would thus show that He takes cognisance of the sins of all His children, even the poorest and least significant in the eyes of their fellowmen. At the same time, Christ is ever available as the sin offering for all believers. Before approaching God in worship, the value of the blood of Christ to cleanse from sin must be appreciated. Before God accepts Christ as the burnt offering from the believer, he must acknowledge his indebtedness to Christ as the sin offering.

The kind of sin requiring an offering is depicted in Leviticus chapter 5 verses 1-4. This is additional to the unwitting sins of chapter 4 verses 2, 13, and 22. While no sin is so trifling in God's sight as to be overlooked, He is gracious and desires to forgive even these lesser transgressions. For some sins, the thunders of the law demanded inexorable judgment, Num. 15. 30. But the sins committed without full knowledge, for refraining from being witness to an oath, for touching an unclean thing, for rash swearing, for these things God held the offender guilty and yet made provision so that by means of an offering the sin could be expiated. In all this God would teach us that sins reckoned small by man's standards are not insignificant in His sight, but would interfere with the believer's proper worship.

The Ritual

The ritual of the sin offering consisted of six actions:

(1) bringing an offering to the door of the tabernacle;
(2) laying hands on the offering, and possibly then confessing the sin, Lev. 5. 5; 16. 21;
(3) killing the offering where the burnt offering was killed;
(4) the priest dealing with the blood – *in the cases of the high priest and the congregation* sprinkling it before the veil, putting it on the horns of the altar of incense, and pouring out the remainder at the base of the brazen altar. *In the case of the others*, putting some on the horns of the brazen altar, and then pouring the rest at its base;
(5) burning the fat on the brazen altar;

(6) disposing of the remainder of the sacrificed animal – *in the cases of the high priest and the congregation* burning all the remnant outside the camp. *In the case of the others* – the priest eating what was left, 6. 29-30.

When birds were presented, the blood of one was sprinkled on the side of the brazen altar and the rest of the blood poured out at its base. The second bird was offered as a burnt offering 1. 15-17. In bringing flour, no oil nor frankincense was added, as in the case of the meal offering, but a handful out of the flour was taken and burned on the altar as a memorial.

Some interesting facts emerge from the consideration of this ritual,

(1) The offering in all cases was brought to the same place, to the door of the tabernacle. There is no distinction among sinners in the sight of God, Rom. 3. 22-23.

(2) The laying of hands on the animal and the confession of sin indicated the offerer's identification with the offering, with the acknowledgement that it would henceforth bear the judgement due to his sin.

(3) The specific mention that the sin offering should be slain where the burnt offering was killed suggests a close relationship between these offerings.

The greater detail concerning the blood of the animal in the sin offering draws particular attention to the shedding of the blood, the giving of the life. It emphasizes the lesson of Hebrews chapter 9 verse 22, that apart from the shedding of blood there is no remission of sins. The sprinkling of the blood of the offering for the high priest and the congregation before the veil reminds us that the sins of God's priests must be atoned for within the holy place, into which alone the priests went. The blood of the offerings for the ruler and the common person was only sprinkled on the brazen altar in the court, to which alone the ordinary Israelite had access. Thus the nearer the sinner approached God, the more intensive must be the expiation.

(4) As in the case of the peace offering all the fat was the Lord's. It was all burnt on the altar as the visible evidence of

divine appropriation of what was best. In this God smelled
a sweet savour,
(5) The burning outside the camp of the remnants of the
animal offered for the high priest or the congregation
reminds us that this was the place where the curse was
borne, Lev. 24. 14-15.

The Truth set forth by the Offering

This sin offering was God's provision for those already sheltered
by the blood of the Pascal lamb. This indicates the believer's need
to appreciate Christ as his sin offering before he approaches God
in worship, or seeks to serve Him, Heb. 9. 14. It portrays not so
much the sinner's initial coming to Christ for salvation, as the provision in Christ for sins committed by the believer in his walk
since conversion. He does well ever to be conscious both of his
sins, even though regenerate, and of his need for cleansing from
them if he is to serve God effectually.

Everyone who sinned, whatever his rank, had to bring his
offering, and kill it at the brazen altar. Every believer, without
regard to his standing in the church, is shut up to the one sin
offering, the death of Christ on the cross: 'the blood of Jesus
Christ his Son cleanseth us from all sin', 1 John 1. 7. Just as the
Israelite, laying his hand on the offering, confessed his sin, so will
the believer find that if he confesses his sins, God is faithful and
just to forgive him his sins.

The sprinkling of the blood within the holy place for the sin of the
high priest or of the priestly nation reminds us that the blood of
Christ avails for us in the holy place in heaven, to which we have
access as priests today, Heb. 9. 12; 10. 19-22; 12. 24. The sprinkling
of the blood was done by the priest. So our heavenly priest today
presents the value of His blood to God as a propitiation for our
sins. To this function He was appointed by God, Heb. 2. 17 RV.

The taking off of the fat, as in the case of the peace offering, and
the burning of it on the altar for a sweet savour to God, indicate
the delight God has in the sacrifice of Christ as our sin offering.
The pleasure of the Lord has prospered in His hand. The burning
of the remainder outside the camp points to the fact that 'Jesus
also, that he might sanctify the people through his own blood,
suffered without the gate', 13. 12 RV. It was outside the city of

Jerusalem, John 19. 20; it was the place of reproach, the place of the outcast of Israel, the ultimate depth of the Lord's humiliation.

When we see Thy love unshaken – outside the camp,
Scorned by man, by God forsaken – outside the camp.

[ELIZABETH DARK]

The law of the sin offering, Lev. 6. 24-30, impresses us with the sanctity with which God regarded it. It must be eaten in a holy place; it must be eaten only by the males; it was put into vessels reckoned holy; it was most holy. And so with the great antitypical sin offering. His was not the offering of 'the shambles'. He was the Holy One, who offered Himself up without blemish for the sins of His people, Heb. 7. 26-27. Let us then appreciate more and more the value of the work of Christ on the cross for our sins. Let us behold Him afresh 'made sin for us'. Let us hasten to avail ourselves of His propitiatory work on behalf of those sins we commit, often so easily, as believers. We do well to recognize these sins, judging them in the light of God's holiness, and not in comparison with the sins of our fellowmen. Let us confess them, and seek forgiveness and cleansing through the blood of His cross – the sin offering that still avails for us today. Then we can go on in the holy exercise of worship.

6. THE TRESPASS OFFERING

In the Levitical economy the sin and trespass offerings were closely associated. Both were for sin, the former emphasizing the sinner's need for cleansing and reconciliation to God, whilst the latter kept prominent the idea of satisfaction for the wrong done. These two offerings were distinct from the burnt, meal and peace offerings in that these latter were sweet savour offerings, whilst the former were essentially intended for the expiation of sin and to secure the offender's restoration to God.

The Hebrew word translated 'trespass offering' in the King James Version and 'guilt offering' in the Revised Version is *asham*. It is used of:

(1) the trespass, Ps. 68. 21;
(2) the trespass offering, Lev. 5. 18; and
(3) the compensation paid for a trespass, 1 Sam. 6. 3.

This word *asham* carries the idea of a default, a wrong done to another, an injury. It is very difficult at times to separate trespass from sin, *chattath*, Gen. 18. 20, for all trespass is sin. Sometimes the terms are used interchangeably, cf. Lev. 5. 6, where, however, 'trespass offering' should be rendered 'for his guilt', RV margin. But it would seem that *asham* is the wrong done, the result, whilst *chattath* is the doing of the wrong, the act.

A trespass is quantitative, Ezra 10. 10, and the trespass offering has to do with those sins in which there is measurable debt. It is concerned not only with atonement and expiation, but also with the reparation for the material damage done to another. It was ordained for a specific type of sin, described as committing a trespass, Lev. 5. 15; 6. 2. In these verses, a different word is used for trespass, one that suggests acting in an underhand manner, implying that the sinner has taken an unfair advantage of another. This trespass was divided into two groups:

(1) in the things of the Lord, 5. 14-19; and
(2) in the things of his neighbour, 6. 1-7.

The trespass in the things of the Lord is further subdivided into:

> (1) things that he should have done but failed to do,
> e.g., the paying of tithes, or of firstfruits, Mal. 3. 8-9,
> (2) something done that he ought not to have done, e.g.,
> eating the fat of the peace offering, or sacrificing unsound
> animals whose blemishes later came to his notice, Mal. 1. 8.
> Idolatry is also described as a trespass under this category,
> 2 Chron. 28. 22-23. This advantage in the things of God had
> been taken unwittingly, as stated expressly, Lev. 5. 15, 18.

Need we remind ourselves that it is possible for believers today to trespass 'in the holy things of God'? We can withhold from God His just demands on our time, purses and energy. These things may be done unwittingly, but we should readily confess them, restoring that which we have denied God and adding a fifth. Christ is our 'ram of the trespass offering', by which our propitiation is made and our sin forgiven.

The nature of the trespass against a neighbour is outlined in Leviticus chapter 6 verses 1-3, as dealing falsely in the matter of:

> (1) a deposit left in his keeping;
> (2) bargaining;
> (3) stealing;
> (4) defrauding;
> (5) stealing by finding; and
> (6) swearing falsely.

In each case the distinguishing feature is the appropriation of what belonged to another. Possibly these trespasses were also done unwittingly, for Exodus chapter 22 verses 1-15 mentions much greater punishments for wilful acts of dishonesty. Note that the trespass against his neighbour was also against the Lord, Lev. 6. 2. Thus, in every case, the ram must be brought to expiate this trespass against God. This offering was essentially an individual offering – a satisfaction rendered to another for wrong done and to God whose law had been broken. It was never offered on holy days nor by the congregation, as was the sin offering.

The Ritual

The ritual of the trespass offering was in two parts:

(1) the confession of the trespass, Num. 5. 7, the assessment
of the damage and its restitution;
(2) the offering of a ram to God.

The assessment was done by the priest, estimating the damage
in silver according to the standard weight of the sanctuary, Lev.
5. 15, the shekel of twenty gerahs. The shekel was a *weight* of
about half an ounce. Not until after 140 B.C. was this term used of
a *coin*. It was the appointed standard by which God's rights were
measured – it seems to have been a heavier shekel than that of the
merchant, Gen. 23. 16, and that of the king, 2 Sam. 14. 26. The
variation in the trespasses was met by the different assessments
of the priest in the amounts to be restored. To this estimation a
fifth was added, and the whole made good to the neighbour who
had been wronged. If, perchance, the offended party had died
since the offence was committed, and had left no heirs, then the
restitution money must be given to the priest, acting on behalf of
God. The adding of the fifth would prevent the wrong-doer gain-
ing any pecuniary or other advantage in retaining the principal
for a time.

Then and only then could the ram be brought. With God there
was no question of forgiveness until a full reparation had been
made. Unlike the sin offering, one animal only could be brought
for a sacrifice in the trespass offering. In the sin offering, there
was a grading of the sacrifice, but in the trespass offering the one
specified sacrifice indicates that there is no respect of persons
with God, Rom. 2. 11. All who have defrauded must make restitution, and, by bringing a ram, must acknowledge that God has
been wronged. This ram must be without blemish, a symbol of
the sinlessness of Christ known to God. The purpose of the sacrifice was to make atonement for the sinner, since in every case the
trespass, whether against God or against his neighbour, was
regarded as unfaithfulness to God, Lev. 6. 2. This is the sense
in which David said, 'Against thee, thee only, have I sinned',
Ps. 51. 4. Even though he had committed a trespass against Uriah,
he had sinned against God, cf. Luke 15. 18, 21. May we thus be
ever conscious that when we trespass against our fellow men we
are sinning against God.

The ram was killed where the burnt offering was slain, on the north side of the brazen altar, Lev. 1. 11. The blood was sprinkled on the altar. In the sin offering the blood was applied with the priest's finger in more elaborate detail. The different ritual in the matter of the sprinkling of the blood arose from the fact that in the sin offering everything affected by the sin must be cleansed. In the trespass offering the reparation of the wrong was the most important feature and the sprinkling lay in the background.

The fat was then removed from the ram, as in the peace and sin offerings, 3. 9; 4. 31. This was burned on the altar – a firing unto the Lord, 7. 3-5. What remained of the animal became the priest's. It was eaten only by males and in the holy place. Like the sin offering the trespass offering was most holy, a term applied to those portions which could be eaten only by the priests, Lev. 2. 3.

The Truth set forth by the Offering

The term *asham* was used prophetically of the sacrifice of the Lord Jesus Christ on Calvary, Isa. 53. 10. The purpose of God had been frustrated by the fall; man had sinned and had trespassed against God, having withheld that which was God's right. God's honour had been injured; His throne had been slighted; His glory had been sullied. But Christ, who ever honoured the Father, more than paid the recompense in His sufferings on the cross. The cross revealed God's throne, God's honour, and God's glory in a way that had never been seen before. There Christ's obedience unto death gave honour to God; His sufferings manifested the glory of God; His enduring the cross vindicated the justice of the throne of God. Hence, the redeemed in eternity will be able to sing of the love of God more fully because of its greater revelation at Calvary.

Christ indeed was the One who for us restored that which He took not away, Ps. 69. 4. Note the use of the words 'much more' in Romans chapter 5. In verse 15, grace abounded much more than the trespass, and, in verse 17, the reign of life is seen to exceed much more the reign of death. Paul sums it up in verse 20, 'where sin abounded, grace did much more abound'. Christ's death met all the satisfaction demanded by the justice of God.

On Calvary, the Lord paid in full the debt that our sins had incurred, but His sacrifice was primarily towards God – to make expiation for us. God assessed our trespasses according to His own standard, 'the shekel of the sanctuary'. That price the Lord

Jesus paid on Calvary. Thus, Christ presented Himself to God as a trespass offering (note the RV margin of Isa. 53. 10, 'when his soul shall make an offering – a guilt offering'). The Lord's experience there was more than a sacrifice, more than death. It was 'the death of the cross', Phil. 2. 8; it was the death that included shame, scoffing, and solitude. He added the fifth on our behalf.

Today we are only too conscious that the believer can commit a trespass and invade the rights of his fellows. He acts falsely in many business dealings; he takes advantage of another's reduced circumstances to drive a hard bargain; he steals his employer's time; he oppresses his employee by withholding his rightful wages, Jas. 5. 4; he fails to restore to its proper owner what he finds. What must he do? The trespass offering would teach him that he cannot expect forgiveness for his sin until he has given satisfaction to him whom he has wronged. Let him confess his trespass, be it ever so humiliating. Let him make amends where possible and more than repay the debt incurred. In making restitution, he must do it according to the teaching of God's word, not accepting the lower standards often allowed by the laws of men. Let him not hide behind the cover of the bankruptcy court which allows a man to compound with his creditors, God's word insists that the whole debt be paid; until that is done reparation has not been fully made. The trespass must be estimated 'after the shekel of the sanctuary'. Then let him present to God as his trespass offering Christ, the Lamb without spot or blemish, the Lamb that beareth away the sin of the world. Thus will he exercise himself 'to have always a conscience void of offence toward God, and toward men', Acts 24. 16.

7. THE DRINK OFFERING

Many of the major offerings of the Levitical economy were accompanied by two of a subsidiary nature, namely, the meal and drink offerings; the latter we shall now consider. The term drink offering, Exod. 29. 40, is the English rendering of the Hebrew *nesek*, a word that comes from a root meaning 'to pour out'. The pouring out of a liquid was a recognized method of propitiating a god among the heathen nations. In Daniel chapter 2 verse 46 the word 'oblation' is, literally, the thing poured out. Thus Nebuchadnezzar ordered that worship be rendered to Daniel. Apostate Israel had copied the practices of the heathen in pouring out drink offerings to false gods, and to the host of heaven, on the tops of their houses, Jer. 32. 29. For this they received righteous retribution from God as He sent the Chaldeans against them. The god to whom the drink offering was offered was said to drink the wine of the offerings, Deut. 32. 38.

The first example of a drink offering is seen in the life of Jacob. In Genesis chapter 35 verse 14, he is described as having 'poured a drink offering' on the pillar of stone that he had erected as a memorial to the occasion when God had talked with him. He used oil for this purpose and thus he expressed his worship of God. On first leaving home, he similarly poured oil on the top of the stone that he had used as a pillow during the night when God spoke to him in a dream, Gen. 28. 18. David also employed such an offering by itself when, on receiving the water from the well at Bethlehem from men who had hazarded their lives to obtain it, he poured it out as an offering unto the Lord, 2 Sam. 23. 16.

The Hebrew *nesek* is used, first, of drink offerings in general, and, secondly, as a technical term for the drink offering of wine which God commanded to be poured out on the burnt and peace offerings – the sweet savour offerings. It does not seem to have been used with either the sin or trespass offerings. The most frequent use of the drink offering in the Levitical ritual seems to have been its application to the burnt offering, where it was intimately associated with the meat offering. Apparently, no burnt offering might be presented without these subsidiary offerings. The omission of the drink offering in Leviticus chapters 1-6 is significant. The explanation is found in Numbers chapter 15 verse 2. It was intended to be implemented only when Israel came into the land, as wine in such prescribed quantities would not be readily available in the wilderness.

The Materials

Various materials were poured out as drink offerings. Jacob poured out oil, the emblem of fatness, as an expression of the abundance that he had received from God. David poured out water, offering to God the service that men had rendered, even their lives which they had risked for David's sake. The psalmist speaks of the drink offerings of blood that idolatrous Israel offered, Ps. 16. 4. Here, blood may mean literal blood, since some offered human sacrifices to Moloch and Chemosh. On the other hand, it may be that blood is put for wine – the blood of the grape, Deut. 32. 14. Or again, the drink offering of blood may be a metaphorical way of expressing the fact that the offerer had hands stained with blood.

God ordained that the drink offering presented to Him should consist of wine, Exod. 29. 40; it was also called strong wine, Num. 28. 7; it was the best that the Israelite used. This wine made glad the heart of man, Ps. 104. 15, but if taken to excess it was intoxicating, Prov. 23. 29-30. Wine, the evidence of the blessing of God, Gen. 27. 28, is used in scripture as an emblem of joy – cheering God and man, Judg. 9. 13. Thus, the drink offering brought joy to God. It was a sweet savour unto the Lord, Num. 15. 7; it was well-pleasing unto Him. In Hosea chapter 9 verse 4, the prophet said that because Israel would fail to offer wine offerings they would cease to please God. The drink offering expressed, too, the pleasure the offerer had in bringing his sacrifice to God. On the other hand, the ill-effects of over indulgence in wine point to it as a symbol of wrath, Rev. 14. 10. This was what the sacrificed animal experienced as it was being consumed by the fire.

The Ritual

There was no elaborate ritual associated with the drink offering. It consisted in the pouring out of the offering. Varying quantities of wine were ordained to be offered with the different sacrifices, Num. 15. 5, 7, 10. With a lamb, a quarter of a hin (about two pints)

was offered; with a ram, a third of a hin (about three pints); with
a bullock, half a hin (about four pints). The differing values of
the offerings upon which these varying quantities of drink offering were poured indicate the different appreciations of the
offerer. Thus, the greater the offering the more joy God received
in the sacrifice.

The quantity was measured in the holy place. Numbers chapter 28
verse 7 describes it as being poured out there unto the Lord. For
this purpose, golden vessels were kept on the table of shew-bread,
Exod. 37. 16; Num. 4. 7 RV. In Numbers chapter 4 verse 7, the word
'covers' (RV 'cups') is the rendering of the Hebrew *nesek*, else-
where translated 'drink offering'. The wine was then poured on
the offering. Some expositors think that the wine was poured on
the brazen altar, because of the prohibition about pouring it on the
altar of incense, Exod. 30. 9. Urijah, in setting up the false altar for
Ahaz, poured his drink offering upon the altar, 2 Kgs. 16. 13. But it
would seem from Leviticus chapter 23 verse 18 that this offering
was poured on the portion of the animal that was burnt; it was
part of the offering made by fire and is often designated as belong-
ing to the sacrifice, Num. 15. 5, 11-12. None of it was drunk by the
priest; it was all for God. The pouring out of the wine denoted the
offerer's devotion to God.

The Truth set forth by the Offering

The drink offering, in common with the other Levitical offerings,
has lessons to teach us concerning the work of the Lord on Calvary. It symbolizes the joy the Father received from the death of
His Son. Christ was ever well-pleasing to the Father, in the work of
creation, Gen. 1. 31; in His incarnation, Heb. 10. 6-9; in His years of
obscurity, Luke 2. 52; 3. 22; in His service, Matt. 12. 18. But from
His death the Father received His greatest pleasure. It pleased
Him that One so capable was willing to bear man's judgement.
With joy the Father raised Him from the dead, exalted Him to the
right hand of the Majesty on High and set Him forth as a propitiation for sins. What a delight the Lord Jesus Christ was to God!

The drink offering also gave expression to the offerer's pleasure.
So Christ was pleased to offer Himself for our sins. He delighted
to give Himself to the Father's will for our redemption, Ps. 40. 8.
Wine as a symbol of wrath prefigured what the Lord Jesus Christ
endured on Calvary, as God poured on Him the wrath that was
our due.

The New Testament teaches us another lesson from the drink offering. Note the Revised Version margin of Philippians chapter 2 verse 17. Here the pouring out is emphasized. Paul writes that if he is 'poured out as a drink offering upon the sacrifice and service' of the Philippians' faith, he rejoices with them. He regarded as a burnt offering the sacrifice and service that their faith called for and his own activity and service on their behalf as the drink offering poured out on their burnt offering. This caused him joy. In the Old Testament, the drink offering sets forth the Israelite's joy in his desire to pour out himself, his strength, his energies for the service of God. This is not so much the pouring out of life unto death, but looking rather to the things of others, as Paul had enjoined, Phil. 2. 4. Thus, in Philippians chapter 2 verse 17 the pouring out implies an action akin to what we find in Romans chapter 12 verse 1, the giving of one's body as a living sacrifice. In 2 Timothy chapter 4 verse 6 RV margin, the pouring out is looked at differently. There it is regarded as the giving of one's life in martyrdom for the cause of Christ. Paul describes the imminence of his death as 'already being poured out as a drink offering'. Thus the apostle not only regarded the use of his life for others as a drink offering, but also the laying down of that life for God.

All this is seen in perfection in the life and death of Christ. In His life He came not to be served, but to serve. His joy was to see His disciples loving one another, John 15. 10-12; He rejoiced in their enlightenment, Luke 10. 21. In His death, too, the Lord Jesus Christ ever had joy set before Him – the joy of bringing many sons to glory. It caused Him to endure the sharpness of the cross and despise its shame, Heb. 12. 2; it caused Him to pour out His soul unto death, Isa. 53. 12.

The experience of the Lord Jesus Christ as pictured in the drink offering is the example for believers today. May we seek joy in pouring out our life's energy and activity for the sake of others, thereby to help them serve and worship God.

We have thus completed our study of the offerings. They have set before us Christ in His various attributes. We have learned to appreciate how His work on Calvary is so very comprehensive and so far reaching in its effects. We see in it the cleansing of the sin offering that prepares us for God's presence. The cross displays the trespass offering making restitution for the debt our sins had incurred. Calvary enables us to worship God. We can present the work of the cross as an adequate burnt offering and know that God will accept it. We apprehend Christ's life as it answers so perfectly to the details of the meal offering. In fellowship with God and with one another, we feast on Christ as a peace offering, on Him who has passed through the fires of Calvary for us. We rejoice in this participation and God smells a sweet savour from it. Let us learn to appreciate more fully the Lord Jesus Christ and His giving of Himself to the death of the cross from the standpoint of the offerings.